Navigating the NIST Cyber Security Framework

A Senior Leader's Guide to Cybersecurity Excellen

Copyright 2023 © Paul Thomas

 https://www.linkedin.com/in/paultthomas/

Printed by: Amazon Kindle Direct Publishing

ISBN: 979-838-8236258

CONTENTS

1. Introduction

The Cybersecurity Landscape

In today's connected world, the importance of cybersecurity cannot be overstated. With an ever-evolving landscape of threats and vulnerabilities, organisations of all sizes are at risk of cyberattacks that can lead to significant financial, operational, and reputational damage. As technology advances and the reliance on digital systems and data grows, the need for robust cybersecurity measures has become a top priority for businesses, governments, and individuals alike.

Cyber threats come in many forms, ranging from state-sponsored cyber espionage and sophisticated hacking groups to individual cybercriminals engaging in identity theft and ransomware attacks. These adversaries are constantly probing for weaknesses in networks, systems, and applications, making it essential for organisations to take a proactive approach in securing their digital assets.

The Importance of Cybersecurity for Senior Leaders

As a senior leader, you play a critical role in shaping your organisation's cybersecurity posture. Your understanding of the risks, commitment to allocating resources, and ability to set the tone for a security-conscious culture can have a profound impact on your organisation's resilience against cyber threats.

Regulatory bodies and investors increasingly recognise the importance of cybersecurity, with many requiring organisations to demonstrate a commitment to safeguarding their digital assets. Failure to prioritise cybersecurity can result in legal and financial consequences, as well as damage to your organisation's reputation and customer trust.

What is the NIST CSF Framework?

The National Institute of Standards and Technology (NIST) Cybersecurity Framework (CSF) is a voluntary, risk-based framework that provides a set of best practices, guidelines, and principles for managing and reducing cybersecurity risk. Developed through collaboration between industry and government, the NIST CSF offers a flexible and scalable approach to cybersecurity that is applicable to organisations of all sizes and industries.

The NIST CSF is built around five core functions: Identify, Protect, Detect, Respond, and Recover. Each function is further divided into categories and subcategories, providing a comprehensive framework for managing cybersecurity risk. By following the NIST CSF, senior leaders can help their organisations build a strong foundation for cybersecurity and ensure they are well-prepared to face the challenges of the digital age.

This book will guide you through the NIST CSF, exploring its components, implementation, and benefits in depth. As a senior leader, you will gain valuable insights and actionable steps to improve your organisation's cybersecurity posture and better protect your digital assets against threats.

2. An Overview of the NIST CSF Framework

History and Development

The NIST Cybersecurity Framework (CSF) was developed in response to Executive Order 13636, issued by President Barack Obama in February 2013, which called for the creation of a voluntary, risk-based cybersecurity framework to improve the security and resilience of critical infrastructure. The National Institute of Standards and Technology (NIST) led the development process, collaborating with various stakeholders from the private sector, academia, and government agencies.

The first version of the NIST CSF was released in February 2014, and since then, it has become a widely adopted and respected framework for managing cybersecurity risks. Organisations across various industries, including financial services, healthcare, energy, and transportation, have found the NIST CSF to be a valuable tool for improving their cybersecurity posture.

Core Functions, Categories, and Subcategories

The NIST CSF is organised into five core functions, each representing a critical aspect of cybersecurity risk management:

Identify: Develop an understanding of your organisation's cybersecurity risks, including the systems, assets, data, and capabilities that need protection. This function helps organisations prioritise their cybersecurity efforts based on their risk profile.

Protect: Implement appropriate safeguards to ensure the delivery of critical infrastructure services and protect sensitive information. This function focuses on access control, data security, and employee training, among other measures.

Detect: Develop and implement monitoring and detection capabilities to identify cybersecurity events in a timely manner. This function emphasises continuous monitoring, anomaly detection, and security event logging.

Respond: Establish and maintain a plan to address cybersecurity incidents when they occur. This function includes incident response planning, communication, analysis, and mitigation.

Recover: Develop and implement strategies to restore affected systems and services following a cybersecurity incident. This function focuses on recovery planning, improvements, and coordination with external stakeholders.

Each core function is further divided into categories and subcategories, which provide a more detailed breakdown of specific cybersecurity activities and objectives. The NIST CSF offers a comprehensive and flexible approach, allowing organisations to tailor its implementation to their specific needs and risk environment.

Benefits of Implementing the NIST CSF

Adopting the NIST CSF can provide a range of benefits for organisations, including:

Improved cybersecurity posture: The NIST CSF offers a structured approach to managing cybersecurity risks, helping organisations identify and address weaknesses in their defences.

Enhanced communication and collaboration: By using a common language and framework, the NIST CSF enables better communication and collaboration between internal teams, as well as with external partners and stakeholders.

Regulatory compliance: Implementing the NIST CSF can help organisations meet regulatory requirements and demonstrate a commitment to cybersecurity best practices.

Increased stakeholder confidence: Adopting the NIST CSF can signal to investors, customers, and partners that your organisation takes cybersecurity seriously, boosting their trust and confidence in your ability to protect sensitive information and critical infrastructure.

Better decision-making: The NIST CSF provides a structured approach to assessing and prioritising cybersecurity risks, enabling senior leaders to make more informed decisions about allocating resources and investments in cybersecurity.

In the following chapters, we will explore each of the NIST CSF's core functions in detail, providing guidance and insights to help senior leaders effectively implement the framework and strengthen their organisation's cybersecurity posture.

3. Implementing the NIST CSF Framework

Understanding Your Organisation's Risk Profile

The first step in managing cybersecurity risks is to understand your organisation's unique risk profile. This involves identifying the key systems, assets, data, and capabilities that must be protected, as well as the potential threats and vulnerabilities that could compromise them.

By developing a clear picture of your organisation's risk landscape, you can prioritise cybersecurity efforts and allocate resources more effectively.

To build a comprehensive understanding of your risk profile, consider the following factors:

Business objectives and priorities: Align your cybersecurity efforts with your organisation's strategic goals and priorities, ensuring that critical assets and operations receive the necessary protection.

Regulatory requirements and industry standards: Assess the specific compliance requirements and industry standards that apply to your organisation, and ensure that your cybersecurity programme addresses these obligations.

Threat landscape: Stay informed about the latest cybersecurity threats, trends, and vulnerabilities that could impact your organisation, and use this knowledge to guide your risk management efforts.

Asset inventory: Maintain an up-to-date inventory of your organisation's hardware, software, data, and network assets, and prioritise protection efforts based on the criticality and sensitivity of these resources.

Assessing the Threat Landscape

To effectively manage cybersecurity risks, you must be aware of the various threats that could target your organisation. These threats can come from a range of sources, including nation-state actors, cybercriminals, hacktivists, and insider threats. Understanding the tactics, techniques, and procedures (TTPs) used by these adversaries can help you better protect your organisation's assets and operations.

Some common types of cyber threats include:

Malware: Malicious software designed to infiltrate, damage, or compromise a system or network, including viruses, worms, Trojans, ransomware, and spyware.

Phishing: Fraudulent attempts to trick users into revealing sensitive information or granting unauthorised access to systems, typically through deceptive emails or websites.

Denial of Service (DoS) attacks: Attacks designed to overwhelm a system or network with excessive traffic, rendering it unable to function properly.

Insider threats: Malicious actions by employees or other insiders, either intentional or accidental, that compromise an organisation's cybersecurity.

Supply chain attacks: Cyberattacks targeting an organisation's suppliers or third-party service providers, potentially compromising the security of the organisation itself.

Tools and Techniques for Risk Identification

To effectively identify and assess cybersecurity risks, organisations can employ various tools and techniques, including:

Vulnerability assessments: Regularly scan your organisation's systems and networks for known vulnerabilities, and prioritise remediation efforts based on the severity of the identified risks.

Penetration testing: Simulate real-world cyberattacks to test the effectiveness of your organisation's defences and identify potential weaknesses that could be exploited by adversaries.

Threat intelligence: Leverage threat intelligence feeds and platforms to stay informed about the latest threat actors, TTPs, and vulnerabilities relevant to your organisation.

Risk assessment frameworks: Adopt risk assessment frameworks, such as NIST SP 800-30 or FAIR (Factor Analysis of Information Risk), to systematically identify, analyse, and prioritise cybersecurity risks.

Incident reporting and analysis: Establish processes for reporting and analysing cybersecurity incidents within your organisation, and use this information to inform your risk management efforts.

In the next chapter, we will explore the Protect function of the NIST CSF and discuss strategies for implementing robust security measures to safeguard your organisation's critical assets and operations.

4. Protecting Your Organisation

Developing a Robust Security Strategy

With a clear understanding of your organisation's risk profile and the threats you face, you can begin to develop a robust security strategy. This strategy should align with your organisation's overall business objectives and encompass a wide range of security controls and measures to protect your critical assets, data, and infrastructure.

Key components of a successful security strategy include:

Governance: Establish a governance structure that defines the roles, responsibilities, and decision-making authority for your organisation's cybersecurity programme.

Policies and procedures: Develop and maintain clear, comprehensive policies and procedures that outline your organisation's approach to cybersecurity and provide guidance for employees.

Risk management: Implement a systematic process for identifying, assessing, and mitigating cybersecurity risks, ensuring that your organisation's security posture remains in line with its risk appetite and tolerance.

Training and awareness: Foster a security-conscious culture by providing regular cybersecurity training and awareness programmes for all employees.

Continuous improvement: Regularly evaluate and update your security strategy to adapt to changes in your organisation's risk environment, technology landscape, and business objectives.

Implementing the NIST CSF Protect Function

The Protect function of the NIST CSF focuses on implementing safeguards to ensure the delivery of critical infrastructure services and protect sensitive information. Key categories within the Protect function include:

Access control: Implement measures to limit access to your organisation's systems, networks, and data based on the principle of least privilege, and ensure that only authorised individuals have access to sensitive information.

Data security: Develop and enforce policies and procedures for securely storing, transmitting, and disposing of sensitive data, and use encryption, tokenisation, or other methods to protect data at rest and in transit.

Network security: Employ network segmentation, firewalls, intrusion detection and prevention systems, and other technologies to protect your organisation's networks from unauthorised access and malicious activity.

Security awareness and training: Educate employees about cybersecurity risks, policies, and best practices, and provide ongoing training to keep them informed about emerging threats and vulnerabilities.

Maintenance: Regularly update and patch software, hardware, and firmware to address known vulnerabilities and ensure that your organisation's systems remain secure.

Protective technology: Implement security technologies, such as antivirus software, endpoint protection, and data loss prevention (DLP) solutions, to help prevent, detect, and respond to security incidents.

Establishing a Security Awareness Culture

One of the most critical aspects of a successful cybersecurity programme is fostering a security-aware culture within your organisation. Employees are often the first line of defence against cyber threats, and their actions can significantly impact your organisation's security posture.

To establish a security-aware culture, consider the following strategies:

Executive support: Demonstrate commitment to cybersecurity from the highest levels of your organisation, setting the tone for the importance of security and fostering a culture of accountability.

Regular training: Provide ongoing cybersecurity training and awareness programmes for all employees, ensuring they understand their roles and responsibilities in protecting your organisation's assets and data.

Gamification and incentives: Use gamification techniques, such as simulated phishing exercises or security quizzes, to make cybersecurity training more engaging and effective. Offer incentives and rewards for employees who demonstrate strong security awareness and behaviours.

Clear communication: Communicate cybersecurity policies, procedures, and best practices in clear, easy-to-understand language, ensuring that employees know what is expected of them.

Learning from incidents: When security incidents occur, use them as learning opportunities to improve your organisation's security posture and reinforce the importance of cybersecurity best practices.

In the next chapter, we will explore the Detect function of the NIST CSF, focusing on the development and implementation of the detection of cyber security events.

5. Detecting Cybersecurity Events

The Importance of Detection

Effective detection capabilities are crucial for managing cybersecurity risks. By identifying cybersecurity events and incidents in a timely manner, organisations can quickly respond and mitigate the potential damage. Early detection can also provide valuable insights into your organisation's security posture and help identify areas for improvement.

The Detect function of the NIST CSF focuses on developing and implementing monitoring and detection capabilities that enable organisations to recognise cybersecurity events as they occur.

Key Components of a Detection Strategy

A comprehensive detection strategy should encompass several key components, including:

Continuous monitoring: Implement continuous monitoring of your organisation's systems, networks, and applications to identify anomalies, suspicious activities, and potential threats.

Security event logging: Collect and analyse logs from various sources, such as firewalls, intrusion detection systems (IDS), and endpoint security solutions, to detect and correlate security events.

Anomaly and threat detection: Use advanced analytics and machine learning techniques to identify unusual patterns or behaviours that may indicate a cybersecurity event.

Security Information and Event Management (SIEM): Implement a SIEM solution to aggregate and analyse security event data from multiple sources, enabling more effective detection and response to potential incidents.

Incident detection and response plan: Develop a plan for detecting, reporting, and responding to cybersecurity incidents, and ensure that all employees are familiar with their roles and responsibilities in the event of an incident.

Implementing the NIST CSF Detect Function

The Detect function of the NIST CSF includes several categories that help organisations establish effective detection capabilities:

Anomalies and events: Establish processes and tools to detect anomalous activities and security events that may indicate a cybersecurity incident.

Security continuous monitoring: Implement continuous monitoring of your organisation's systems, networks, and data to identify potential threats and vulnerabilities.

Detection processes: Develop and maintain formalised detection processes that enable your organisation to identify cybersecurity events and incidents in a timely manner.

To implement the Detect function effectively, consider the following steps:

Assess your current detection capabilities: Evaluate your organisation's existing monitoring and detection tools, processes, and technologies to identify gaps and areas for improvement.

Define detection requirements: Establish clear objectives and requirements for your organisation's detection capabilities, taking into account factors such as regulatory requirements, industry standards, and your organisation's risk profile.

Select and deploy appropriate tools and technologies: Choose detection tools and technologies that align with your organisation's needs and objectives, and ensure they are properly configured and integrated with your existing systems.

Establish processes for event analysis and correlation: Develop processes for analysing and correlating security events, leveraging tools such as SIEM solutions to help identify potential incidents and prioritise response efforts.

Train employees and stakeholders: Provide training and awareness programmes to ensure that employees and other stakeholders understand their roles and responsibilities in detecting and reporting cybersecurity events and incidents.

In the next chapter, we will explore the Respond function of the NIST CSF, focusing on strategies for effectively addressing and managing cybersecurity incidents when they occur.

6. Responding to Cybersecurity Incidents

The Need for an Incident Response Plan

No organisation is immune to cybersecurity incidents, and having a well-defined incident response plan is essential for minimising the potential damage and recovering quickly. An effective incident response plan can help organisations contain and mitigate threats, protect sensitive information, and maintain business continuity during and after an incident.

The Respond function of the NIST CSF focuses on establishing and maintaining a plan to address cybersecurity incidents when they occur.

Key Components of an Incident Response Plan

A comprehensive incident response plan should include the following key components:

Roles and responsibilities: Clearly define the roles and responsibilities of your incident response team, including team members, stakeholders, and external partners.

Communication protocols: Establish communication protocols for notifying stakeholders, including employees, customers, partners, and regulators, during and after an incident.

Incident classification: Develop a classification system for categorising incidents based on their severity, impact, and required response actions.

Incident response procedures: Document step-by-step procedures for each phase of the incident response process, including detection, containment, eradication, recovery, and post-incident review.

Incident reporting and documentation: Implement processes for documenting and reporting incidents, including the collection and preservation of evidence for potential legal or regulatory actions.

Implementing the NIST CSF Respond Function

The Respond function of the NIST CSF includes several categories that help organisations establish effective incident response capabilities:

Response planning: Develop and maintain a comprehensive incident response plan that outlines your organisation's approach to addressing cybersecurity incidents.

Communications: Establish processes and procedures for coordinating internal and external communications during and after an incident, ensuring that stakeholders receive timely and accurate information.

Analysis: Analyse the nature and scope of incidents, including the identification of affected systems, data, and infrastructure, as well as the potential impact on your organisation's operations.

Mitigation: Implement measures to contain and mitigate the impact of incidents, including the isolation of affected systems, the removal of threats, and the implementation of additional security controls.

Improvements: Conduct post-incident reviews to identify lessons learned and opportunities for improvement, and update your incident response plan and processes accordingly.
To implement the Respond function effectively, consider the following steps:

Develop your incident response plan: Create a comprehensive plan that addresses the key components outlined above, and ensure that it is regularly reviewed and updated to remain relevant and effective.

Establish an incident response team: Form a dedicated team of trained and qualified individuals who are responsible for managing and executing your organisation's incident response plan.

Conduct regular training and exercises: Provide regular training and conduct simulated incident exercises to ensure that your incident response team and other stakeholders are prepared to respond effectively to real-world incidents.

Integrate with detection and prevention efforts: Ensure that your incident response plan is closely integrated with your organisation's detection and prevention capabilities, enabling a seamless transition from detection to response in the event of an incident.

Review and update your plan: Conduct post-incident reviews and use the lessons learned to continuously improve your incident response plan and processes.

In the next chapter, we will explore the Recover function of the NIST CSF, focusing on strategies for restoring affected systems and services and building resilience in the face of future incidents.

7. Recovering from Cybersecurity Incidents

The Importance of Recovery and Resilience

Recovering from a cybersecurity incident is a critical step in minimising its impact and returning to normal operations. An effective recovery strategy ensures that affected systems and services are restored quickly and securely, reducing downtime and the potential for further damage. Building resilience into your organisation's infrastructure and processes can also help prevent future incidents and improve your overall cybersecurity posture.

The Recover function of the NIST CSF focuses on developing and implementing plans for restoring systems and services affected by cybersecurity incidents and building resilience to minimise the impact of future incidents.

Key Components of a Recovery Strategy

A comprehensive recovery strategy should include the following key components:

Recovery planning: Develop and maintain a plan for restoring affected systems and services following a cybersecurity incident, including processes for data backup, recovery, and restoration.

Business continuity: Establish processes and procedures for maintaining critical business functions during and after an incident, ensuring that your organisation can continue to operate effectively.

Disaster recovery: Develop a disaster recovery plan that outlines the steps and resources required to restore your organisation's infrastructure and operations following a major incident.

Lessons learned: Conduct post-incident reviews to identify lessons learned and opportunities for improvement, and use this information to update your recovery plans and processes.

Resilience planning: Implement measures to strengthen your organisation's infrastructure and processes, reducing the likelihood and impact of future incidents.

Implementing the NIST CSF Recover Function

The Recover function of the NIST CSF includes several categories that help organisations establish effective recovery capabilities:

Recovery planning: Develop and maintain a comprehensive plan for restoring systems and services affected by cybersecurity incidents.

Improvements: Continuously improve your organisation's recovery capabilities by incorporating lessons learned from previous incidents and implementing measures to enhance resilience.

Communications: Establish processes for coordinating internal and external communications during the recovery phase of an incident, ensuring that stakeholders receive timely and accurate information.

To implement the Recover function effectively, consider the following steps:

Develop your recovery plan: Create a comprehensive plan that addresses the key components outlined above, and ensure that it is regularly reviewed and updated to remain relevant and effective.

Integrate with your incident response plan: Ensure that your recovery plan is closely integrated with your organisation's incident response plan, enabling a seamless transition from response to recovery in the event of an incident.

Conduct regular training and exercises: Provide regular training and conduct simulated recovery exercises to ensure that your organisation is prepared to execute its recovery plan effectively in the event of an incident.

Review and update your plan: Conduct post-incident reviews and use the lessons learned to continuously improve your recovery plan and processes.

Build resilience: Implement measures to strengthen your organisation's infrastructure and processes, reducing the likelihood and impact of future incidents.

In conclusion, the NIST CSF provides a comprehensive framework for managing cybersecurity risks, encompassing the Identify, Protect, Detect, Respond, and Recover functions. By following the guidance and best practices outlined in this book, senior leaders can develop and implement a robust cybersecurity programme that aligns with their organisation's strategic objectives and risk profile, and effectively safeguards critical assets and operations.

8. Maintaining and Improving Your Cybersecurity Programme

The Need for Continuous Improvement

In the rapidly evolving world of cybersecurity, organisations must continually adapt and evolve their security programmes to address emerging threats and changing business requirements. A successful cybersecurity programme requires ongoing maintenance, review, and improvement to remain effective and aligned with your organisation's strategic objectives and risk profile.

In this final chapter, we will explore strategies for maintaining and improving your cybersecurity programme, ensuring its long-term success and resilience.

Key Components of Continuous Improvement

A comprehensive approach to continuous improvement should include the following key components:

Regular risk assessments: Conduct periodic risk assessments to identify new threats, vulnerabilities, and changes to your organisation's risk profile.

Policy and procedure reviews: Review and update your organisation's cybersecurity policies and procedures to ensure they remain relevant, effective, and aligned with industry best practices.

Technology updates and upgrades: Keep your security technologies up to date by regularly updating and patching software, hardware, and firmware, and consider upgrading or replacing outdated systems as needed.

Training and awareness: Provide ongoing cybersecurity training and awareness programmes for all employees, ensuring they remain informed about emerging threats, vulnerabilities, and best practices.

Performance measurement and reporting: Establish performance metrics and reporting processes to track the effectiveness of your cybersecurity programme, identify areas for improvement, and demonstrate progress to stakeholders.

Incident response and recovery lessons learned: Conduct post-incident reviews to identify lessons learned and opportunities for improvement, and use this information to update your incident response and recovery plans and processes.

Implementing a Continuous Improvement Process

To implement a continuous improvement process for your cybersecurity programme, consider the following steps:

Establish a governance structure: Develop a governance structure that provides oversight and direction for your organisation's cybersecurity programme, ensuring accountability and clear decision-making authority.

Set performance objectives and metrics: Define clear performance objectives and metrics for your cybersecurity programme, enabling you to measure progress, identify areas for improvement, and demonstrate success to stakeholders.

Conduct regular reviews and audits: Perform periodic reviews and audits of your organisation's cybersecurity programme, including risk assessments, policy and procedure reviews, and technology assessments, to identify gaps and areas for improvement.

Identify and prioritise improvements: Use the results of your reviews and audits to identify and prioritise improvements to your cybersecurity programme, ensuring that resources are allocated effectively and improvements are aligned with your organisation's risk profile and strategic objectives.

Implement and monitor improvements: Implement the identified improvements, and monitor their effectiveness using your established performance metrics and reporting processes.

Foster a culture of continuous improvement: Encourage a culture of continuous improvement within your organisation, promoting an ongoing commitment to cybersecurity best practices and resilience.

By following the guidance and best practices outlined in this book, senior leaders can develop, implement, and maintain a robust cybersecurity programme based on the NIST CSF framework. Through continuous improvement, organisations can adapt to the ever-changing cybersecurity landscape, ensuring the long-term success and resilience of their cybersecurity programme.

9. Engaging Senior Leadership in Cybersecurity

The Role of Senior Leadership in Cybersecurity

In today's interconnected world, cybersecurity is not just an IT issue; it is a critical business risk that affects every aspect of an organisation. Senior leaders, including executives and board members, play a vital role in establishing and maintaining a robust cybersecurity programme. Their engagement, support, and commitment are essential for ensuring the long-term success and resilience of the organisation's cybersecurity posture.

In this chapter, we will explore strategies for engaging senior leadership in cybersecurity and ensuring that they understand the importance of their role in managing cybersecurity risks.

Strategies for Engaging Senior Leadership

To effectively engage senior leadership in cybersecurity, consider the following strategies:

Communicate the business impact: Clearly articulate the potential business impact of cybersecurity risks, including financial losses, reputational damage, regulatory penalties, and operational disruptions.

Align cybersecurity with strategic objectives: Demonstrate how a robust cybersecurity programme supports your organisation's strategic objectives, such as protecting intellectual property, maintaining customer trust, and ensuring business continuity.

Use clear and concise language: When communicating with senior leaders, avoid technical jargon and use clear, concise language that focuses on business risks and outcomes.

Present metrics and key performance indicators (KPIs): Develop and present metrics and KPIs that provide a clear picture of your organisation's cybersecurity posture and the effectiveness of your cybersecurity programme.

Regularly report on cybersecurity: Establish a regular reporting cadence to keep senior leaders informed about the organisation's cybersecurity risks, progress, and challenges.

Engage in ongoing education and training: Encourage senior leaders to participate in cybersecurity education and training programmes, ensuring they remain informed about emerging threats, vulnerabilities, and best practices.

Include cybersecurity in board meetings: Include cybersecurity as a regular agenda item at board meetings, ensuring that it receives the attention and oversight it deserves.

Building a Cybersecurity Culture from the Top Down

Senior leadership sets the tone for an organisation's culture, and their commitment to cybersecurity is essential for fostering a culture of cybersecurity awareness and resilience. By demonstrating a strong commitment to cybersecurity, senior leaders can help create an environment where all employees understand the importance of protecting the organisation's digital assets and are empowered to take action to mitigate risks.

In conclusion, the engagement and support of senior leaders are critical for the success of any cybersecurity programme. By following the strategies outlined in this chapter, organisations can effectively engage their senior leadership in cybersecurity, ensuring their commitment to managing cybersecurity risks and fostering a culture of cybersecurity awareness and resilience.

10. Building a Cybersecurity Ecosystem

The Importance of Collaboration and Partnership

In the complex landscape of cybersecurity, no organisation can afford to tackle challenges in isolation. Collaborating with external partners, such as industry peers, government agencies, and third-party vendors, can help organisations share knowledge, resources, and best practices, resulting in a stronger and more resilient cybersecurity ecosystem.

In this chapter, we will explore strategies for building partnerships and fostering collaboration within the cybersecurity community, enhancing your organisation's overall security posture.

Strategies for Building Partnerships and Collaboration

To effectively collaborate and build partnerships within the cybersecurity community, consider the following strategies:

Participate in industry forums and associations: Join industry-specific forums and associations that focus on cybersecurity, providing opportunities for networking, information sharing, and collaboration with peers facing similar challenges.

Engage with government agencies and initiatives: Collaborate with government agencies and participate in initiatives that promote cybersecurity awareness, information sharing, and cooperation between the public and private sectors.

Establish information sharing agreements: Develop formal information-sharing agreements with trusted partners, outlining how threat intelligence, vulnerabilities, and best practices will be shared to enhance collective cybersecurity efforts.

Leverage third-party expertise: Engage third-party vendors and consultants who specialise in cybersecurity to provide additional expertise, resources, and support for your organisation's security programme.

Collaborate on research and development: Partner with academic institutions, research organisations, and other industry players to collaborate on research and development efforts aimed at advancing cybersecurity knowledge and solutions.

Attend and participate in cybersecurity conferences and events:
Regularly attend and participate in cybersecurity conferences and events, which offer valuable opportunities for networking, learning, and collaboration.

Building a Strong Cybersecurity Ecosystem

Organisations can enhance their overall security posture and bolster a more resilient cybersecurity ecosystem by promoting collaboration and forming partnerships within the cybersecurity community. This approach offers several significant advantages, such as:

Enhanced threat intelligence: Sharing threat intelligence among partners enables organisations to identify and respond to emerging threats more effectively and efficiently.

Improved best practices: Collaborating with external partners can help organisations identify and adopt best practices, enhancing their cybersecurity programme's effectiveness.

Access to additional resources and expertise: Partnerships can provide organisations with access to additional resources and expertise, supplementing their internal capabilities and helping them address complex cybersecurity challenges.

Greater resilience: A collaborative cybersecurity ecosystem enables organisations to collectively respond to and recover from incidents more effectively, reducing the potential impact on individual organisations.

In conclusion, building partnerships and fostering collaboration within the cybersecurity community is essential for enhancing your organisation's overall security posture and contributing to a more resilient cybersecurity ecosystem. By following the strategies outlined in this chapter, organisations can effectively collaborate with external partners, benefiting from shared knowledge, resources, and best practices to strengthen their cybersecurity defences.

11. Future Trends and Challenges in Cybersecurity

The Evolving Cybersecurity Landscape

The cybersecurity landscape is constantly evolving, driven by rapid technological advancements, the changing threat landscape, and the growing interconnectedness of our digital world. To stay ahead of emerging threats and protect their organisations, senior leaders must remain informed about future trends and challenges in cybersecurity.

In this chapter, we will explore some key trends and challenges that organisations may face in the coming years, providing insights to help senior leaders prepare for the future of cybersecurity.

Key Future Trends and Challenges

The rise of artificial intelligence (AI) and machine learning: As AI and machine learning continue to advance, they will play an increasingly important role in both offensive and defensive cybersecurity strategies. Organisations must stay ahead of these technological developments, adopting AI-powered security solutions while being aware of the potential for AI-driven cyberattacks.

The expanding Internet of Things (IoT): The growing proliferation of IoT devices presents new challenges for cybersecurity, as these devices often lack strong security measures and can serve as entry points for cybercriminals. Organisations must implement robust IoT security strategies to protect their networks and data.

Increasing regulatory and compliance requirements: As governments and regulators worldwide continue to focus on cybersecurity, organisations must be prepared to meet evolving compliance requirements, such as data protection and privacy laws.

The growing importance of data privacy: Consumer concerns about data privacy are driving organisations to adopt more stringent data protection measures. Senior leaders must ensure that their organisations prioritise data privacy and implement appropriate security controls to protect sensitive information.

Supply chain and third-party risks: As organisations become more interconnected, they become increasingly vulnerable to supply chain and third-party risks. Organisations must implement comprehensive vendor risk management programmes and continuously monitor the security posture of their partners.

The expanding threat landscape: Cyber threats continue to evolve, with cybercriminals adopting new tactics and techniques to exploit vulnerabilities. Organisations must stay informed about emerging threats and invest in advanced detection and response capabilities to protect their assets and operations.

Preparing for the Future of Cybersecurity

To stay ahead of the evolving cybersecurity landscape, senior leaders must take a proactive approach to addressing future trends and challenges. Consider the following strategies:

Invest in emerging technologies: Stay informed about emerging cybersecurity technologies and invest in solutions that can help your organisation stay ahead of new threats and vulnerabilities.

Prioritise workforce development: Develop a skilled cybersecurity workforce by investing in training, education, and professional development programmes.

Foster a culture of cybersecurity awareness: Encourage a culture of cybersecurity awareness and resilience throughout your organisation, ensuring that all employees understand their role in protecting the organisation's digital assets.

Continuously assess and adapt your cybersecurity programme: Regularly assess your organisation's cybersecurity programme, adapting to emerging trends and challenges to maintain a strong security posture.

Collaborate with external partners: Strengthen your organisation's cybersecurity ecosystem by fostering collaboration and partnerships with external partners, such as industry peers, government agencies, and third-party vendors.

In conclusion, the future of cybersecurity presents both challenges and opportunities for organisations. By staying informed about emerging trends and proactively addressing future challenges, senior leaders can ensure that their organisations remain resilient and well-prepared to navigate the complex cybersecurity landscape.

12. Conclusion and Key Takeaways

The Critical Role of Cybersecurity in the Modern Business World

In the modern business world, cybersecurity is a crucial element for organisations of all sizes and industries. As technology continues to evolve and the digital landscape expands, the need for robust cybersecurity programmes will only grow. Senior leaders play a vital role in establishing and maintaining effective cybersecurity programmes, ensuring that their organisations are well-prepared to address the challenges and risks of the digital age.

Throughout this book, we have explored the NIST CSF framework, providing guidance and best practices to help senior leaders develop and implement a comprehensive cybersecurity programme that aligns with their organisation's strategic objectives and risk profile.

Key Takeaways

As we conclude, let's revisit some key takeaways for senior leaders:

Understand the importance of a strong cybersecurity programme: Recognise the critical role of cybersecurity in protecting your organisation's assets, operations, and reputation.

Utilise the NIST CSF framework: Leverage the NIST CSF to develop a comprehensive and flexible cybersecurity programme that addresses the Identify, Protect, Detect, Respond, and Recover functions.

Engage senior leadership and foster a cybersecurity culture: Encourage the engagement of senior leaders in cybersecurity and foster a culture of cybersecurity awareness and resilience throughout the organisation.

Regularly assess and improve your cybersecurity programme: Continuously assess your organisation's cybersecurity posture and implement improvements to address emerging threats, vulnerabilities, and evolving business requirements.

Collaborate with external partners: Build partnerships and collaborate with external partners to strengthen your organisation's cybersecurity ecosystem and share knowledge, resources, and best practices.

Stay informed about future trends and challenges: Remain informed about emerging trends and challenges in cybersecurity, ensuring that your organisation is well-prepared to navigate the ever-changing cybersecurity landscape.

By following the guidance and best practices outlined in this book, senior leaders can effectively address the challenges and risks of the digital age, safeguarding their organisation's assets, operations, and reputation. The NIST CSF framework provides a solid foundation for developing and maintaining a robust cybersecurity programme, enabling organisations to achieve long-term success and resilience in an increasingly interconnected world.

13. Assessing Maturity with NIST CSF and Implementation Tiers

Introduction

The NIST CSF assists organisations in assessing and improving their cybersecurity posture through a structured and risk-based approach. The Framework Implementation Tiers are a valuable tool to measure cybersecurity maturity and align risk management practices with industry standards and best practices. This chapter will discuss the scoring process using the Framework Implementation Tiers and explain how organisations can use this approach to evaluate their cybersecurity maturity.

Understanding the Framework Implementation Tiers

The NIST CSF Implementation Tiers are divided into four levels, representing the organisation's maturity level in implementing the NIST CSF practices. The tiers are:

Tier 1 - Partial
Tier 2 - Risk-Informed
Tier 3 - Repeatable
Tier 4 - Adaptive

It is essential to note that the tiers are not meant to be a one-size-fits-all solution.

Organisations should adopt the tier that best aligns with their specific risk tolerance, resources, and business environment.

Scoring the Organisation's Cybersecurity Maturity

To assess an organisation's cybersecurity maturity using the NIST CSF Implementation Tiers, follow these steps:

Review the organisation's current cybersecurity risk management practices across the five Framework Core Functions: Identify, Protect, Detect, Respond, and Recover.

Compare the organisation's existing practices with the guidance provided in the NIST CSF, focusing on the Categories and Subcategories within each Function.

Assign a maturity level (Tier) that reflects the organisation's implementation status based on the comparison.

Identify areas for improvement by analysing gaps between the organisation's current practices and the recommended practices in the NIST CSF.

Develop an action plan to address the identified gaps and improve the organisation's cybersecurity maturity.

Using the Implementation Tiers to Assess Cyber Maturity

Organisations can leverage the Implementation Tiers to evaluate their cybersecurity maturity and identify areas for improvement.

Establish a baseline: Determine the organisation's current cybersecurity posture by assessing its existing risk management practices across the five Framework Core Functions. This baseline provides a starting point for measuring progress and improvement.

Choose the appropriate tier: Select the tier that best aligns with the organisation's risk tolerance, resources, and business environment. This tier will serve as the target maturity level for the organisation's cybersecurity programme.

Identify gaps: Compare the organisation's current cybersecurity practices with the recommended practices in the NIST CSF to identify gaps and opportunities for improvement.

Develop an action plan: Create a roadmap for improving the organisation's cybersecurity maturity by addressing the identified gaps. This plan should include clear objectives, timelines, and resources required for each improvement initiative.

Monitor progress: Regularly review and update the organisation's cybersecurity practices to track progress towards the target maturity level. This process should involve continuous monitoring, evaluation, and adjustment of the cybersecurity program based on the evolving threat landscape and the organisation's changing needs.

In the following tables, each NIST CSF domain and subcategory is listed, followed by the tier assessment for each subcategory. The Implementation Tiers are indicated by their corresponding number: Tier 1 - Partial, Tier 2 - Risk-Informed, Tier 3 - Repeatable, and Tier 4 - Adaptive.

NIST CSF Domain: Identify

Subcategory	Tier 1 – Partial	Tier 2 - Risk-Informed	Tier 3 - Repeatable	Tier 4 - Adaptive
Asset Management	Asset inventory incomplete, and classification not established	Asset inventory established, and classification in progress	Asset inventory complete, and classification well-defined	Asset inventory and classification continuously updated
Business Environment	Cybersecurity roles and responsibilities not defined	Cybersecurity roles and responsibilities defined but not consistently applied	Cybersecurity roles and responsibilities integrated into the organisation's governance structure	Cybersecurity roles and responsibilities continuously updated based on emerging threats
Governance	Cybersecurity risk management practices ad hoc	Cybersecurity risk management practices documented but not consistently applied	Cybersecurity risk management practices integrated into the organisation's governance structure	Cybersecurity risk management practices continuously updated based on emerging threats
Risk Assessment	Risk assessments not comprehensive, and risk management practices ad hoc	Risk assessments performed based on a defined methodology, and risk management practices documented	Risk assessments conducted periodically, and risk management practices integrated into the organisation's governance structure	Risk assessments performed continuously, and risk management practices regularly updated based on emerging threats
Risk Management Strategy	Risk management strategies not well-defined	Risk management strategies established, but not consistently applied	Risk management strategies well-defined and integrated into the organisation's processes	Risk management strategies continuously updated based on emerging threats
Supply Chain Risk Management	Supply chain cybersecurity risks not identified	Supply chain cybersecurity risks identified but not consistently addressed	Supply chain cybersecurity risks integrated into the organisation's risk management program	Supply chain cybersecurity risks continuously monitored and addressed

NIST CSF Domain: Protect

Subcategory	Tier 1 – Partial	Tier 2 - Risk-Informed	Tier 3 - Repeatable	Tier 4 - Adaptive
Access Control	Access controls inconsistent and not documented	Access controls documented and based on a risk-based approach	Access controls consistently applied and tested periodically	Access controls adapted based on the evolving threat landscape
Awareness and Training	Awareness and training programs not established	Awareness and training programs in progress	Awareness and training programs regularly updated and tested	Awareness and training programs continuously improved based on feedback and predictive indicators
Data Security	Policies and procedures related to data security not established	Policies and procedures related to data security established but not consistently applied	Policies and procedures related to data security well-established and integrated into the organisation's processes	Policies and procedures related to data security continuously updated based on emerging threats
Information Protection Processes and Procedures	Protection processes and procedures not established	Protection processes and procedures established but not consistently applied	Protection processes and procedures consistently applied and periodically tested	Protection processes and procedures continuously improved based on emerging threats
Maintenance	Protective technology not maintained	Protective technology maintained, but not regularly updated	Protective technology regularly maintained and updated	Protective technology continuously updated based on the latest security vulnerabilities
Protective Technology	Protective technology not in place	Protective technology in place but not regularly tested	Protective technology regularly tested and maintained	Protective technology continuously tested and improved based on feedback and emerging threats

NIST CSF Domain: Detect

Subcategory	Tier 1 – Partial	Tier 2 - Risk-Informed	Tier 3 - Repeatable	Tier 4 - Adaptive
Anomalies and Events	Anomalies and events not systematically detected	Anomalies and events detected, and security continuous monitoring in progress	Anomalies and events detected through a formalized process that is consistently applied	Anomalies and events detected through a continuous and adaptive process that leverages machine learning and artificial intelligence
Security Continuous Monitoring	Security continuous monitoring not established	Security continuous monitoring in progress	Security continuous monitoring established and integrated into the organisation's security operations centre	Security continuous monitoring adaptive and continuously improves based on emerging threats
Detection Processes	Detection processes ad hoc and inconsistent	Detection processes established, but not consistently applied	Detection processes well-documented and periodically tested	Detection processes continuously updated based on feedback and predictive indicators

NIST CSF Domain: Respond

Subcategory	Tier 1 – Partial	Tier 2 - Risk-Informed	Tier 3 - Repeatable	Tier 4 - Adaptive
Response Planning	Response planning not established	Response planning in progress	Response planning established and integrated into the organisation's incident response program	Response planning continuously improved based on emerging threats and lessons learned
Communications	Communication during a cybersecurity incident limited	Communication during a cybersecurity incident improving	Communication during a cybersecurity incident consistent and documented	Communication during a cybersecurity incident proactive and shared with external partners
Analysis	Analysis of incidents ad hoc and inconsistent	Analysis of incidents well-documented but not consistently applied	Analysis of incidents consistently applied, and the root cause analysis is documented	Analysis of incidents leverages machine learning and artificial intelligence to identify patterns and trends
Mitigation	Mitigation activities not well-defined	Mitigation activities established, but not consistently applied	Mitigation activities well-defined and integrated into the organisation's risk management program	Mitigation activities continuously updated based on emerging threats and feedback

NIST CSF Domain: Recover

Subcategory	Tier 1 – Partial	Tier 2 - Risk-Informed	Tier 3 - Repeatable	Tier 4 - Adaptive
Improvements	Improvements after an incident not well-documented	Improvements after an incident documented, but not consistently applied	Improvements after an incident consistently applied and integrated into the organisation's risk management program	Improvements after an incident leverage machine learning and artificial intelligence to identify areas for improvement
Recovery Planning	Recovery planning not established	Recovery planning in progress	Recovery planning established and integrated into the organisation's business continuity plan	Recovery planning continuously improved based on emerging threats and lessons learned
Improvements	Improvements after an incident not well-documented	Improvements after an incident documented, but not consistently applied	Improvements after an incident consistently applied and integrated into the organisation's risk management program	Improvements after an incident leverage machine learning and artificial intelligence to identify areas for improvement
Communications	Communication after a cybersecurity incident limited	Communication after a cybersecurity incident improving	Communication after a cybersecurity incident consistent and documented	Communication after a cybersecurity incident proactive and shared with external partners

14. Epilogue - Embracing a Cyber-Resilient Future

As we conclude our exploration of the NIST CSF framework and its application to senior leadership, it is essential to look beyond the present and embrace the future. The digital age has brought about remarkable advancements, opportunities, and challenges, and the cybersecurity landscape will continue to evolve rapidly.

In this epilogue, we will reflect on the importance of embracing a cyber-resilient future and the steps senior leaders can take to ensure their organisations are prepared for the challenges ahead.

The Journey Toward Cyber Resilience

Developing and maintaining a comprehensive cybersecurity programme is not a one-time effort; it is an ongoing journey that requires constant vigilance, adaptation, and improvement. As senior leaders, it is crucial to recognise that achieving cyber resilience is a long-term commitment that involves continuous efforts to protect and adapt to an ever-changing threat landscape.

To embrace a cyber-resilient future, senior leaders should:

Champion cybersecurity at the highest levels: Ensure that cybersecurity remains a top priority for the organisation, with strong support and commitment from senior leadership and board members.

Adapt to emerging trends and technologies: Stay informed about the latest cybersecurity trends, threats, and technologies, and be prepared to adapt your organisation's cybersecurity programme accordingly.

Foster innovation and collaboration: Encourage a culture of innovation and collaboration within your organisation, promoting the development of new ideas, approaches, and solutions to address evolving cybersecurity challenges.

Invest in the cybersecurity workforce: Attract, develop, and retain a skilled cybersecurity workforce by providing ongoing training, education, and professional development opportunities.

Emphasise the importance of risk management: Recognise that cybersecurity is an essential component of enterprise risk management and ensure that your organisation's risk management processes adequately address cybersecurity risks.

Preparing for an Uncertain Future

The future of cybersecurity is filled with uncertainty, as new threats, vulnerabilities, and technologies continue to emerge. However, by embracing a cyber-resilient mindset and following the guidance outlined in this book, senior leaders can help their organisations navigate this uncertain landscape with confidence.

As we look to the future, it is essential to remember that the most successful organisations will be those that remain agile, adaptive, and resilient in the face of ever-evolving cybersecurity challenges. By fostering a strong cybersecurity culture, investing in the necessary resources, and leveraging the NIST CSF framework, senior leaders can ensure that their organisations are well-prepared to confront the challenges of the digital age and build a more secure and resilient future.

15. Appendix A: Glossary of Key Terms and Acronyms

CISO: Chief Information Security Officer - A senior executive responsible for developing and implementing an organisation's cybersecurity program.

CSF: Cybersecurity Framework - A framework developed by NIST to help organisations manage and reduce cybersecurity risks.

IAM: Identity and Access Management - A set of processes, technologies, and policies used to manage digital identities and control access to resources.

IoT: Internet of Things - A network of interconnected physical devices that communicate and exchange data with each other.

KPI: Key Performance Indicator - A measurable value that demonstrates the effectiveness of an organisation in achieving key objectives.

NIST: National Institute of Standards and Technology - A U.S. federal agency that develops technology, metrics, and standards to drive innovation and economic competitiveness.

SOC: Security Operations Centre - A centralised unit responsible for monitoring, detecting, responding to, and mitigating cybersecurity incidents.

Resources and References

NIST Cybersecurity Framework:
https://www.nist.gov/cyberframework

NIST Special Publication 800-53:
https://csrc.nist.gov/publications/detail/sp/800-53/rev-5/final

Center for Internet Security (CIS) Critical Security Controls:
https://www.cisecurity.org/controls/

ISO/IEC 27001: Information Security Management:
https://www.iso.org/isoiec-27001-information-security.html

16. Appendix B: Case Study and Best Practices

Scenario: A large insurance company is considering adopting the NIST CSF to strengthen its cybersecurity program, manage risks more effectively, and better align its cybersecurity practices with industry standards and regulatory requirements.

NIST CSF Domain: Identify

Asset Management	Create and maintain an inventory of all hardware, software, and data assets, including their locations and ownership, to ensure proper management and protection of sensitive policyholder information
Risk Assessment	Conduct regular risk assessments to identify, analyse, and prioritise potential cybersecurity risks based on the organisation's risk appetite and tolerance.
Governance	Establish a cybersecurity governance structure that defines roles, responsibilities, and reporting lines for cybersecurity management and oversight within the insurance company.

NIST CSF Domain: Protect

Access Control	Implement role-based access control policies to limit access to critical systems and data to authorised personnel only, ensuring protection of policyholder information.
Data Protection	Protect sensitive data at rest and in transit using encryption, tokenisation, or other appropriate data protection methods, complying with data privacy regulations.
Security Awareness and Training	Develop and deliver ongoing cybersecurity awareness and training programs for employees to improve their understanding of cybersecurity risks and best practices related to the insurance industry.

NIST CSF Domain: Detect

Continuous Monitoring	Implement a continuous monitoring program to detect potential cybersecurity incidents by analysing logs, network traffic, and system events within the insurance company's infrastructure.
Anomaly Detection	Deploy advanced analytics and machine learning tools to identify unusual patterns or behaviours that may indicate a security incident affecting the insurance company's systems or policyholder data.
Security Operations Centre (SOC)	Establish a dedicated SOC to centralise the monitoring, detection, and analysis of potential cybersecurity incidents within the insurance company.

NIST CSF Domain: Respond

Incident Response Plan	Develop and maintain a comprehensive incident response plan that outlines roles, responsibilities, and procedures for responding to cybersecurity incidents affecting the insurance company.
Communication and Coordination	Establish processes for coordinating and communicating with internal and external stakeholders, including law enforcement and regulatory agencies, during a cybersecurity incident.
Analysis and Containment	Implement processes for analysing and containing cybersecurity incidents to minimise their impact on the insurance company and its policyholders.

NIST CSF Domain: Recover

Recovery Planning	Develop and maintain a recovery plan that outlines the steps and resources needed to restore normal operations following a cybersecurity incident affecting the insurance company.
Lessons Learned	Conduct post-incident reviews to identify lessons learned and opportunities for improvement in the insurance company's cybersecurity program.
Continuity of Operations:	Ensure the insurance company's critical business functions can continue during and after a cybersecurity incident by implementing robust business continuity and disaster recovery plans.

By implementing the NIST CSF across these five domains, the insurance company would be able to create a comprehensive and effective cybersecurity program that helps manage and reduce its overall cybersecurity risks while protecting policyholder information.

www.ingramcontent.com/pod-product-compliance
Lightning Source LLC
Chambersburg PA
CBHW061055050326
40690CB00012B/2631